CSU Poetry Series XX

Magic Shows

Poems by David Graham

Cleveland State University Poetry Center

ACKNOWLEDGMENTS

BELOIT POETRY JOURNAL: "Census"

CINCINNATI POETRY REVIEW: "Exits on the Drive Home"

GEORGIA REVIEW: "Landscape of Domestic Life"

IOWA REVIEW: "Paul Celan," "Worcester, Next Nine Exits"

LOUISVILLE REVIEW: "Elegy at Sea"

MONTANA REVIEW: "Mr. In-Between"

NIMROD: "Testament of Arnaud du Tilh"

NEW ENGLAND REVIEW: "Cow Country," "Father Movies"

NEW ENGLAND REVIEW AND BREAD LOAF QUARTERLY: "How Straight Up is Curved"

PANACHE: "What Is Coming"

PASSAGES NORTH: "Crickets in August"

PIEDMONT LITERARY REVIEW: "A Sermon in Stone"

POETRY: "American Gothic," "Dusk," "The Editorial We," "A Lot of Boys Bar," "The Outskirts of Everything"

POETRY NORTHWEST: "In Praise of the Coelacanth"

SOUTHERN POETRY REVIEW: "The Bad Season Makes the Poet Sad," "Clay's Gun" (as "Clay"), "Here Was Buried Thomas Jefferson," "The Scholar Gypsy: a Progress Report"

SPECTRUM: "Descent" (as "We Are All Very Strange")

WORCESTER REVIEW: "Bad Taste Visits Home"

The cover drawing, by Lee Shippey, is based on photographs of the author's grandfather, the Jim of this volume's title poem (pp. 87-92). Cover design by Lee Shippey.

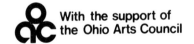

With the support of the Ohio Arts Council

for my mother and father,
Nora Knox Graham
and George A. Graham, Jr.

CONTENTS

I. Census

DUSK

It is the hour between dog and wolf
and the hour of liver spots enlarging
on the soft forearms of my grandmother.
At such times the cinderblocks shrink
into the vacant lot rubble.
It is the hour when the retired
consider part time jobs.

At meals everywhere conversation lags,
the hour between mortar and brick,
between ice cube and tumbler.
In the backyards ropes hang still
from the stripped crotches of trees.
A bad time to encounter mirrors
or ease down into a scalding tub.

When my past comes to inhabit me
it is now the hour of sand,
climbing the stairs step by step
even as I sleep.
Hour of severed phones ringing
and my father who calls me
before him in his night chair.

LANDSCAPE OF DOMESTIC LIFE

The bacon was carved thin
as a lesson, to be taught
by nervous elders
whose every movement
became a skill,
like calming animals.

Some paychecks were good
for buying more checks, fathers
using sons to make grandsons,
pitching themselves
lifelong into that debt.
Sticky butterknives passed

hand to hand down the long table,
still our breakfast smalltalk
revolved always
around the silent center —
fish your own hole,
fish your own hole.

For children the curfew horn meant
the helpless have no business
being stupid. So we found our way home
across unlit yards,
through pried cellar windows,
to pillows asleep in our forms.

THE SCHOLAR GYPSY: A PROGRESS REPORT

The bulletin boards are thick with plaintive notes:
lost cats answering to no name at all,
rewards for wallets, mandolin lessons,
but worst of all, and unattainable,
nonsmoking vegetarian roommates.
In this town leases read "now,"
and landlords have seen enough to know
you'll most likely depart in a bad way,
paid in advance. But our favorite word is "OK,"
and no one's afraid to read the small print,
so this is a town quick with apartments,
students eyeing faculty across the halls.
Do we grow more tolerant? I fear we grow worse,
privy to each other's coughings and flushings,
quirks like the downstairs neighbors',
who play the same record each morning loud,
or my own whistling at birds from the balcony.
I'd challenge a mockingbird if need be.
I learn things, though, in a college town:
next door all day calypso, and upstairs,
commands hurled at a parrot learning French.
All the janitors sing Duke Ellington
and reread Thoreau on their lunch breaks.
At my age my parents had a house, dog,
lawn big enough for a football game, and me.
I live somewhat eerily at the threshold
of one decade, thinking of another.
"For Sale" signs on the road to work
draw my wheel aside like a wayward compass.
There is no lease long enough to age in.
Yet with morning glories on the balcony,
tomatoes blooming in an easily carried pot,
this season begins to look tolerable.
Look: a deaf family is moving in next door;
they have no hobbies and they never cook.
I feel their great dismay rob me of my own.

SEA TURTLE

Deep in your oyster-size brain
is a hatred for sharks,
hunger for jellyfish and crabs,
perfect memory for the sands
of the hatching beach.

You're bad luck, with that barnacle mouth,
plucking ice age sponges
from bottom mud, nearsighted cooter
of the coral reefs. They say
you drum a storm on boat decks.

But you'll die lunging after plastic bags,
jaw thick with fishhooks
you've eaten the bait from.
Your young will crawl toward the light
they think is moonlit sea —

pavement glittering with headlights.
A jeep will eat the eggs
ghost crabs cannot find. You'll butt
your nose raw on aquarium walls,
snap dangled fingers like snailshells.

With breath so foul the shrimp-men gag,
a limitless gut, carapace
sharp to slice their nets
and free a day's catch, you're swimming
to beaches that have washed away.

They say turtle steak won't rest
in the pan, that it takes you
a week to die. They have seen you,
three-legged from old shark bites,
climb crookedly out of the surf

straight into a poacher's machete.
They have seen you headless, dropping eggs.

AT THE ARBORETUM

Most picnics clustered near the gates,
where oxidized scrollwork promised
all trees of noblest kind.
Deeper in were glass-laced hills.

From there the skyline was strangled blue.
A crow fled the arborvitae squawking,
while dogs ran everywhere: in labelled trees,
splashing in culverts without fever or fear.

I said I knew the look of a dog,
when he was harmless, when he would bite.
She said, feel a dog's neck sometime —
they are too strong for comfort.

A couple on the opposite slope
lay tangled in their jackets, their hair.
I couldn't stop watching. I said,
if I were a dog I'd sniff them.

And get kicked in the teeth, she said,
unless you were heartless and quick.
I am very quick, I said,
and she said, we're both heartless.

BAD TASTE VISITS HOME

You can't stop me — I'm
going to talk about bad taste,
the kind your parents have,
with their dreadful trousers
and doggerel plaques,

with their crappy ideas
of fun — such as easy listening,
such as church suppers,
with their required slide shows
of Disneyland looking as cheap

as it ought to be, and yes,
there you always are
centered in such fun,
licking at your ice cream,
trying to look sardonic.

I knew I'd find you
in these overexposed snaps
full of walking cartoons
with fixed, goofy grins —
terrible as novocaine,

sunlight and bad color.
Yet while I'm at it
I'd better talk of loyalty,
the kind you feel, beyond
logic, for parents dead

or alive. Why such duty?
Why the twice-a-year visits,
which you dread, the five pounds
you gain avoiding politics,
avoiding God and grandchildren?

Why isn't it love, too,
this loyal and shuffling duty?
Or is love the bad taste
that makes duty tolerable,
that walks the dog,

admires garish wallpaper,
drinks corkless wines?
Nothing now will stop me
from admiring the creases
in your father's pants

as he kneels to retrieve
your dropped letter; or
the final way your mother
clamps a lid to the pot,
as if steam were formed

of fondness itself. I notice
every food coupon
and sharpened pencil
of your former home,
all the decorations

that outlive holidays,
crosswords half done,
a sliced apple awkwardly set
on an end table and forgotten,
as if the telephone had rung.

Now your Dad mumbles
his mild mistrust
of the new Korean paperboy,
now your Mom recites again
the story of your difficult birth.

Soon it's time for bed,
your twinless twin
where you first dreamed
a house in such guilty taste
it was built entirely of words.

So you climb the stairs
two at a time, more
host than guest now,
and whether in hope or sadness
not even I can tell.

SPARE CHANGE: BOSTON

1. *Museum*

Sailboats flounder in cracked seas
off Scotland, some icefed ocean.
The caste mark on a passing forehead
bores into gaping eyes. Beautiful women
pause before paintings of beautiful women,
or stoop to pat the marble greyhound.
All that the sea can carry it carries.

2. *Street*

A dog behind glass snaps at his own reflection.
Mallards drift headless in the parkpond weeds.
In a dark market, money is stashed overnight
beneath cuts of liver and shining pork.
There's no spare change in any till,
but each corner has its king. Here,
gathering applecores and brown lettuce
to offer the cop's horse, stands a man
so meek he jumps when the subway squeals.

3. *Home*

Who delivers arias to the dumpster?
Let blown leaves build around his legs,
let the fire escape hum.
They drink too much on the fourth floor
and next door they ride the bed hard.
Across the court someone buys every song.
Gulls overhead ride the warmest air.

THE MIND OF A SMALL TOWN

Taillights of a sedan driven by habit
vanish over a hill as night begins
to infiltrate the gullies, ditches, and
hedges of this town where no one famous
has ever visited. A young woman
who is free all night to invent her life
imagines herself on television,
slimmer and smiling into the eyes
of an actor her mother met years back
in an elevator in Chicago.
If it seems that "the mind is its own place,"
even in this small town named for a large one
in another country, the mind *is* its
own place, rutted and washed out like spring roads,
criss-crossed with conflicting messages, like
a map with its overlapping claims.
The woman thinks suddenly of her brother,
out later than he should be, who just now
cups a firefly in one hand and won't show
anyone, not even himself, for fear
it will escape. He sees a floodlight on
a distant house as it buzzes, turns pink,
then gradually grows to blinding white.
What is not seen may not exist, he thinks,
and decides to ignore his sister's call
when it comes. She'll keep time to her own life.

CRICKETS IN AUGUST

A husband sleeps through anything —
fire next door, a late son
drunk on the stairs, dog getting sick —
but he cannot sleep alone.

A wife remembers how many eggs
are in the refrigerator door,
her daughter's grades from high school,
every adrenalin alarm.

Together they make a home
with its inclusions and exclusions.
Bowed floorboards sing one tune
for years in various keys.

And a housekey erodes with use,
long years of hand oil darken it
so that even locks may be fooled —
"Yesterday it worked, I used it."

Saturday, the driveway is full
of a clean car getting cleaner.
The hose, thrown to one side,
turns footsteps in the lawn silver.

And it is summer such a long time
in hedges, grass, and under shade trees
that even crickets are forgiven,
those ceaseless thermometers.

A marriage loses heat with age,
repeats itself, wanders, and won't be rushed —
"A true statement is almost always
longer than a false one."

THE PALMIST

— *for Carl Little*

She pulls my hand across the table
devoting her mouth to each finger in turn.
I tell her I love the grain of wood
beneath her drink, the way
knots mimic water in a drain,
a face photographed by surprise.
She tells me her love for wood newly cut,
still alive at the center,
the face of one falling asleep.

I tell her my father never touched me,
that her hands could never mother mine,
that gifts left in public are gifts to yourself.
She says she tried to scald and rub
the first hair from between her legs;
and the many lies her father told,
holding her close toward the day
she would gladly leave him.

She kisses my palm with her whole face,
while I tell her my father
locked the bookcases until I was sixteen,
and everything I read I read out loud.
Music not allowed, how the piano keys
were one broad smile beneath their cover,
yellowing as ivory does without sun.

AERIAL VIEW

Plowed fields from the air look silver:
Mathew Brady's battlefields,
where blood takes on its true color
and legs of frozen soldiers

lengthen with shadows.
In a black-and-white photograph
this man without caption could be mad,
convulsive, or savoring a sneeze.

Several wars on, hemmed in
with too many heads in the snapshot
I am too fond of close-ups,
suicides in mid-air, lyrical surgery,

and the sheer eye of creation.
With scissors and an arctic squint
I release any man from any woman,
I alter ground and root.

From high enough I should begin to see
Johnny Appleseed prowling the interstate,
Andersonville green as Yosemite,
while from the acid bath the wounded rise.

DESCENT

Grandmothers begin calling
to upstairs neighbors
dead in the fire of 1930.
For years the camera stutters,
then issues a clear command.
You never can tell
when your dog will rouse
to growl all night
at the open window.
Sometimes drunk you see
a darkening in the face of a friend,
and you want to sit all night
on a rock singing —
want to watch death happen,
with the quiet of rain
falling through the air,
watch it come down from the attic,
electric ball down carpeted stairs
and out the front door.
When you blink you are apt
to be hustled down the gangplank
in New York, ashamed
of your accent and heavy shoes,
or you may simply stop your car,
get out, and vanish
into the factories torn down yesterday.
These glimmerings
of all there is to know —
perhaps tonight you will find
the single condom in your father's drawer,
far back under the socks
and cracked with age.

AGAINST DIOGENES

Diogenes, my dog philosopher,
I have to report many loaves of bread
improperly won, eaten as avidly
as before, among the circling cynics
of our day. It pains me very little
to stand in anyone's light, great or small,
though I admit these words to me are bread.
Meet me at the junction of Diode
and Dionysius, in the afterhours
card catalog. Regale me with your scorn
as I memorize your features, not your words.
Thump your tub to deafen great Alexander —
the sound will carry in my genes, won't it?
Already I have learned to drink water
from my hands, and the bitterness of silence.
It is not enough. I could sleep on dirt
and howl like a dog, I could reject
even you as a luxury, and that
could not be honesty enough. The dust
you are I shall soon be, and like the great
Alexander, I miss the point, thinking
that great and good ought to be separate.
But, good cynic, good dog of my library,
I have to report the usual mess
roiling my genes, and wonder what to call
a feeling your lantern never aimed at.
If truth is wind, love is earth — heavy and
corruptible. I have to report eyes
that take on any color rejected
are not mine, and the dust lodged in your eyes
is the land that still holds us together,
our dogs yelping on cue like little clocks.

MR. IN-BETWEEN

Horse laugh of a car that won't start,
then the sullen drum of one that won't stop:

in between a whole junkyard gleams
harsh as a dropped fork,

a stopped pocketwatch getting fat.
Night sweat in the day of streetlights,

single-eyed cruiser blinking,
muffled radio cough. A backdoor swings

drunkenly, and yellow eyes
tighten, a tomcat in the hedge.

Listen, I don't trust a crushed headlight,
handkerchief turning red,

the sound of metal complaining.
The wreck never over, I yell

time out to the mockingbird
trying out a siren in the fruit trees.

In her bedroom, sitting up
by an overshaded lamp, a girl listens

to her father teach a song he likes:
Stop on red, go on green,

don't you mess with Mr. In-Between.
I want to run my hands over metal

crumpled upon itself, make faces
to the diamonds in the grass.

A clock somewhere chimes
the shelf loose from its wall,

a line I can walk all night.
Highway drone used to calm a boy,

while his mother rationed doubts
one to a child, her laundrybag

full of mendable socks, enough
to break the back of a kitchen table.

Slopped with gin, tonight she savors
one lit wall, voices in the street —

I'm circling oddly about her house,
a kite made stubborn by its cut string.

THE CHAIN

Think of Jim Nelson of Knoxville Tennessee
Who turned away a legal jackpot.
You rise from the bottom of the list.
Eight thousand people just like you

Who turned away a legal jackpot —
Nine days later they died.
Eight thousand people just like you.
Let's laugh all the way to next week.

Nine days later they died.
But a dollar will make us rich —
Let's laugh all the way to next week,
Like people with half a brain.

But a dollar will make us rich.
You're right to be skeptical.
Like people with half a brain
You count your friends on one hand.

You're right to be skeptical.
Think of Jim Nelson of Knoxville Tennessee.
You count your friends on one hand.
You rise from the bottom of the list.

WHAT IS COMING

Childhood was a chore
you escaped with plots and silence.

The felled tree that you loved
fathered in its shadow

soft white plants. Your fear
of new friends appeared as a rock

you rubbed with your thumb
until it shone. Where was Mother?

She crept like a toad from the muck,
wearing your face.

*

Imagine a desk, some mail,
and a phone going off in a drawer.

Imagine this mirror as one eye
that will not blink,

no matter what it is shown.
Imagine your own life-line —

see it drift in and out as voices do
half-heard across a courtyard.

*

When it comes you will know
by the palm lines appearing on plates,

the empty pot on your stove
boiling its air to thick steam.

You may call it the Middle
and live it through, riding numbly,

clinging to the stone in your stomach
as you plunge down. When it is over

you will know it is never over,
as behind every hill

someone always looks up,
scanning the slope you cannot see.

CENSUS

Small town evenings
of darkened leathermills
and glove shops.
The jackhammers are still.
Along the old train bed
boys gather at dusk
to throw gravel
at each other. No backhoes
carve holes in vacant lots.
They rise coolly into the air —
a cat in the weeds
may sniff gently
at a tiretread.
Along the shaded sidewalks
at midnight, a lone couple moves
arm in arm, neither old
nor young.

II. How Straight Up Is Curved

HOW STRAIGHT UP IS CURVED:
HOMAGE TO EMILY DICKINSON

— for Joe Donahue

1. "Who Goes to Dine Must Take His Feast"

The way a horse knows,
the moment he is reined around a bend,
that it is home now to the barn,
I feel the car shiver around me and quicken.
Ears of corn just beyond my taillights
begin to tremble in my wake.
Roadsigns seem familiar, then true,
and finally sympathetic.
I know that over this crest, surely,
in a house set back behind maples
a light is on in an upstairs window.
I know that house I have never seen:
bats and nighthawks flash
across the window light, and if she sees
she is fixed as I am fixed
in this landmark of my arrival.

2. "Of Men Escaping From the Mind of Man"

I hear the neighbor's band saw starting,
dog barking at the paperboy —
I hear the impossible fog of dawn.
Clocks hesitate before continuing,
and sheets heavy with night-sweat cling.
Traffic is finally soothing in fog,
this mist from belowground,
where all things are memorable.
I see fog loves the ground,
hovering on any bush planted too far
from a building. I see the feeling
of homecoming on one man's face
as he descends to the street.
A siren cuts the fog apart,

but fog regathers, easily
as water splashed from a puddle,
trees rustling on a road without trees.

3. "How News Must Feel When Travelling"

The ice came down, chunks big as cars,
so beautifully that to admire was to die
and to die was inevitable. This day

the earth swallowed a child, a bad boy
who peered down an abandoned well,
who tortured a cat and then lied,

who tried to outrun the highway.
People lay on floors, people closed eyes
and hung on while the earth shifted.

Only a few could eat, those who knew
something or nothing at all.
And the plane came down in flames,

rupturing the oceanic dream,
urging the sea to open again
as it had in scripture, but this wrong

was too colossal to be made right.
The pilot was in error, his first,
for he had a drink, for he dozed away,

for he nosed down into cooling waves.

4. "This World is Not Conclusion"

For sacrament I have description —
this Sunday crowd milling on Church Street,
a broken shopwindow with weakened alarm,
a traffic light blinded by the sun.

In this world the testament's broken
like glass across an intersection —
and yes, this world is fictional,
column to column, its syntax permanent.

And when this world concludes
it will be Sunday from rumpled front page
to the comics bleeding over my hands.
It will be final as a misprint.

How can any house continue?
The scatter of clocks explaining
fractions to each other, dead weight
of a lover shifting in sleep.

So dream talk is given off,
wrapped in this deep laugh of fear,
concluding in the dusty brilliance
of daylight upon the bedclothes.

5. "If the Stillness is Volcanic in the Human Face"

Volcanic as precision forgetting itself,
so that we may say, *he's blown his top,*
as when a once raging man
settles into kindness, and we say,
he's calm, he's tame, as if
these things were not achievements.
A hundred clicks and groans
enliven the night house,
sounds of adjustment, not protest
or acceptance. No need to rage
if it's so deep in you
that anyone intrigued enough could see.
Nothing is so vicious to endure.
Behind glass or a well-sunk fence
a dog will attack most anyone,
even his own frightened reflection.

6. "Water is Taught By Thirst"

Here above five flooded villages
stone walls emerge from the waves,
old stumps break loose from vanished yards
to bob up polished as bones. I read carved stone
in the graveyard of this reservoir.

When a father gathers his son
under the arms and lets him dangle toes
through the ripples, fish rise.
I look up to see sky lapping,
clouds pale as trout bellies.

As in the day when any town
circumscribed all its lives,
and time had two speeds — the walk
and the run — as in the sunrise
uncomplicated with sleep,

as in the days when couples posed
in straight-back chairs before the cow,
as I too would have lingered here
to withstand the sound of water
in this place of gathering water....

7. "It's Coming — the Postponeless Creature"

Hawk shadow over a well-mowed field,
platonic as a guidebook silhouette;
yet in that passionless soaring
a shape for the rodent genes....

Will the fieldmouse flinch at this shape
it has never seen before?
That gob of nerves, scooting forward
without rattling the milkweed pods,

must be a match for the strangeness
of a shadow that comes
sudden as a hand of dismissal.
Yet whiskers cannot feel the visitor.

And soft as scent the rain falls,
barely calming the yellow weeds,
lightly as breath on a mirror
the binocular hawk descends.

8. "Drowning is Not So Pitiful as the Attempt to Rise"

I wouldn't like to see balloons
released to the sky — their helium blaze
surmounting the trees, tentative
in gusts but relentlessly rising.
It would be shock to see
how straight up is curved,
how even the air is humped high
like the earth in its hills,
like the very arch of space.
Such balloons never fall to earth whole,
for by the time they rise halfway
to the limit, they burst
from unimpeded success,
and begin falling in tatters,
nearly unrecognizable. Or so
they say who have seen it.
I wouldn't like to see it,
or say that I had seen it.

HERE WAS BURIED THOMAS JEFFERSON

"Mountain-built with peaceful citadel" — Keats

On Jefferson's little mountain
we tourists shift from foot to foot
fingering cameras, standing
in a loose democratic line
stretched from shuttle bus to front door.
It's an American prospect:
we who deny royalty come
in our uniform foreign cars
to gawk at this great man's estate,
polite, attentive to tour guides,
accepting the limitations
of velvet rope and forbidden
stairways. We marvel at his life —
but more at his gadgets and the cash
it took to make them than the wit
he spent investing in power.

"With what majesty," he wrote,
"do we there ride above the storms!"
Storms! even at Monticello....
On this hot July afternoon
when soda machines are empty
as the decanters on his shelves,
cardinal flowers are blooming
along the serpentine walkways,
where babies squint, mothers brush flies,
and fathers refold handkerchiefs.

There's no majesty in the crush
toward the air-conditioned great hall.
We shuffle among trophies that
Lewis and Clark carried the breadth
of our country to lay at his feet:
mastodon bones, buffalo head,

antlers of elk and moose, maps of
pure conquest.

                    We agree: this is
no nickel and dime citadel.
We agree: not one of us here
is a descendent of the slaves
this statesman liked to call "servants,"
even as he wrote on the evils
of bondage. This isn't their shrine.
The slave quarters and all manner
of messy "dependencies" are
ingeniously hidden from view
according to the master's plan,
while Mr. Jefferson's office
and flowerbeds surmount the hill.

Such ferocious distinctions would
give anyone migraine headaches,
even as kind a slavemaster
as Tom Jefferson was said
to be. We won't hear from our guides
of the red-haired slave children, or
anything but the classical
verities of this bankrupt farm.
We will hear of Napoleon,
Lafayette, and the miracles
a practical mind can think of.

Forgive me, Tom Jefferson, but
it seems I cannot forgive you
for your genius falling short of
perfection. In your dining room
you installed a revolving shelf
so that your servants could serve you
without being seen. Two dozen
of them joined the British army
in hope of freedom.

I'd rather
leave you unseen in my pocket,
useful to feed parking meters,
or leave you slouched in some corner
with a book on fertilizers,
than peering with patrician eyes
over the throngs of citizens
drawn to your unworkable home.

THE HELPLESS MAKE GOOD COMPANY

In the corridor of a public home
he lived without home, without vote
he lived in a stairwell listening.
He heard voices on a radio waver and merge
to one voice, which is static, which is Babel.
He heard praise and blame, violin bows
that rise and fall in unison. Then the radio
skipped a decade backward, to the time
he would sing every hit, even slumped
stupidly near a conquered bottle.
He heard photos behind glass dissolving,
become transparent, become glass
and worse than glass, windows scored with prints.
He heard the troubled nightly phonecalls
of vague friendship, distant houselights
where hard to locate dogs howled.
He heard prices too low to be mentioned
on that radio, and he believed them.
He heard, on the faintest verge of the dial,
where want ads come to life as likeable women,
the first sputter of oncoming storm,
and he made it welcome.

"THE BAD SEASON MAKES THE POET SAD"

— Herrick

The bad season of ice, TV crackling,
every neighborhood quiet and cold
as the space between electrons. An optimist
must lodge downstairs, humming to the knocks
in the pipes, reading his paper by ruin light.
Here is no sadness, unless the downed wire,
scorching dead grass, can be called sad
more than senseless. I punctuate such a day
with praises, glad if not optimistic.
I praise soft boots printing their names in snow,
praise the faces in the frosted glass.
Yet trusted pipes burst to flood the stairwell,
and a racket fills my windowpanes.
Though I may say this is good, a testing,
bones soften like ice, the wind descends,
and even the thermostat grows doubtful.
Each morning I pray to my car,
bless its battery, and scrape ice from its skin.
Well cooked sausage lingers as dream,
causing the family dog a twitching sleep.
Even the airwaves are thick with worry,
some kind of hunger addressing itself.
This bad season makes me sad only
to calculate its sum, the chatter and gloom
of every distinguished spokesman.

IN PRAISE OF THE COELACANTH

Plain, inexplicable things —
mitochondria and chloroplasts —
we call dim engines of life,
and it's true, you know it's true.

Mice with excised brains continue
pondering electrical grids,
relentless little forgeries
like the valley fog which is not fog.

Van Meegeren, a crooked Dutchman,
sold his fake Vermeer to the Nazis,
who paid him in phony currency —
which is true, you know it's true.

Faces of the saints develop
on bathroom tile, on bread baked
by honest women — such collusion
between motive and surprise.

A century ago, a sailor
tattooed Jesus and Mary on his back
to ward off the deserved whip,
which it didn't, you know it didn't.

Today I read, by the light
of my single gaudy text, miracles —
that there are stones which call out
in voices of the dead;

And devoted ones who bleed
without wound, from hand and foot.
But a counterfeit Lazarus gapes
from every newsstand, you know he does.

No one less photogenic than coelacanth,
fish deeper than we have been,
dragon-scaled throwback with dim brain,
who heaves along the bottom muck,

ferocious and slow in those iron depths.
They say this fish escaped the ark
out of the sheerest good luck —
which is true, you know it's true.

MR. AND MRS. PAIN

— for Dennis Finnell

All my towns, you say, are the same town.
This one, then, on a late August morning,
rain keeping traffic sad down the unschooled,
narrow cobbled streets. We talk of childhood

theatrics, the time you put a live hen
in a tumble dryer, time I cracked a tooth
exploding bottles. A woman in brown
advances, dabs one sleeve to her left eye,

recently bruised. Embarrassing to witness
her shame: like a crossing guard I knew,
Mrs. Something, a grammar school ghost.
Friendly as youth, she knew all our names

but forgot one day her own admonishment.
Clipped by a car, too lame for work, she became
dutiful Mrs. Pain, sending cheerful,
badly rhymed couplets to the less fortunate.

She took as mission the discovery of grief,
and is welcome still, for all I know,
at St. John's Episcopal, where what she gives
has a secret sound, hitting bottom

in the brass collection plate. Like her, I
let memory be faith by default. Yet
don't even nightmares work by analogy?
Aren't we God's crude comparisons?

My friend, we've met these sidewalk people before.
They know us. Like smoke, like wind, like nothing
we'll seep into the cracks and inhabit
this place from inside out. What town

doesn't love its washouts, with crackpot pride
in each crippled dream? We overhear a song
whose question turns to statement: *Don't believe
I'm leaving? You can count the days I'm gone.*

"THE SWEET HELL WITHIN"

— Whitman

The unearthly child of this house
is crib happy, barely whimpers
when hungry, loves mother and father
properly and by name. Her tantrums heal
out of sight like the fontanelle.

Father peddles drugs she never needs,
mother's a nurse doubly off duty.
"She doesn't cry?" says an aunt.
Caterpillars in the backyard maples
ease their daylong rain.

She is peaceful as plumbing all night,
dreaming, we guess, of helium balloons
ascending restlessly, the one sight
that we know can take her breath away.
We huddle in the hope of dim children.

We dream her blessed with no blessing,
and the slow traffic of digestion
her final killer. On the back porch
two aunts and an uncle swap tales
of childhood calculus, knowing

that the egotism of infancy
seldom dies. As the overdue dark
comes on, a civilized clink of ice,
this baby adored in absentia —
we bask in our own devouring.

A SERMON IN STONE

Because everything, even the brass of a trumpet
or a crow's bill, is constantly burning,
and because the moving spruces are shaped like fire
from their crests to their knobby roots,
and because even water in its extremities

scalds and alters the innocent face,
creasing and chastening it like a hillside,
because, in short, the pitiful lung-engine works
and will work — this deaf sister tosses in her crib
noisier than I thought deaf girls should be.

If she is angry we cannot blame her,
but what if she's merely ornery? She likes her hands
and we are told to encourage their flutterings —
see how we make her clap and trill those fingers
to encourage us, her partisans.

As this child imagines death a still mother
and the future a set of fatherly instructions,
and as these things are both false and true,
she wails all morning like the radio next door
and at night just stares at the pilot light.

I plan increasingly to call her dimness happy.
Her future passes swiftly behind like a wake,
foams and eddies, perfectly familiar.
From wisps of Mom's hair to Dad's nicotine nails,
every swirling element lives and burns.

THE EDITORIAL WE

We love the Law, we love the Prophets.
We love what falls between,
dust unwilling to be made flesh
and vice versa. We are fond of Hebrew
in its rolling, translated cadence,
its desire to say everything twice.
When night comes we cower and pray,
we raise our voices in muddy chorus
praising praise our spiritual glue.
It's unfortunate, we know, but our minds
are resolved: there will be no children
darting about our services like misplaced pets.
Children, for as long as they can,
refuse like a curfew the language we dote on.
They are relentless as any law,
less open to reason than the testament,
but in time we solve them. We dress them
as tiny versions of themselves,
we predict with astonishment their success.
If they decide to love, it is ours,
if there is any crime, from the unforgiveable
to the charming, we feel more than certain
that we are at the bottom of it.

MAYBE A GRAVE IS JUST
A HOLE IN THE GROUND

Maybe the dead are just wrong
Like a postcard announcing a child.
They cry wolf and mean it,
The unattractive dead.

Like a postcard announcing a child
As perfect, a nail never driven,
The unattractive dead
Stiffen without strength or plan.

As perfect as a nail never driven,
This final headache. Grief
Stiffens without strength or plan.
It is a stunt gone all wrong,

This final headache, grief
Whistling like boiled snails.
It is a stunt gone all wrong,
Liquor that makes the sad sadder.

Whistling like boiled snails
In the dark familiar room,
Liquor makes the sad sadder,
Doing no harm. But vanishing

In the dark familiar room,
Maybe the dead are just wrong.
Doing no harm but vanishing
They cry wolf and mean it.

POSTCARDS

Each postcard came from a ruined town —
motels, views of caged pools and parking lots.
She wouldn't sign her name, or say
how she acquired mine, but I could guess
the age of each message by the cars
in the background, fins and archaic chrome.
It was mail from my mother's life,
and my grandmother's. She never
told her age, though I thought she knew
the decay of each town personally,
as she wrote stringent comments
on each one's pride in itself,
local beers and queens of the major crop.
After years her cards tapered off —
a few jackalopes, fur-bearing trout,
some antique courthouses
"from before anyone was born."
Nothing, she said, was worth
complaining about anymore.
She went to zoos to see timberwolves
stalk ruts in cage cement,
she grew hysterical at towns
swallowed by good taste, too timid
for a tractor pull or circus.
By the time I figured what she wanted
the cards had stopped, but I sent her news
anyway, addressed to a name in the book.
I told her my life had gone wrong
through every fault of my own.
I told her how hard I took
the under-the-table games of children,
how cats disturbed me with their composure.
My second-to-last card
described a seven-alarm fire
at the house next door — how I watched

the past rise in silhouette, sofas,
pillows blackening to cinders,
and water running brown from our well
for two days, until the rain
that would not come came.

TEN MINUTES OF SILENCE FOR JOHN LENNON

Death by signature, by the hand of love,
All to bring music to bear on murder.
Ten minutes of silence for John Lennon,
Stillness from Liverpool to Adelaide.

All to bring music to bear. On murder
There is little disagreement:
Stillness from Liverpool to Adelaide,
Music heard in scratched grooves by heart.

There is little disagreement
When some rush the stage to be nearer
Music heard in scratched grooves by heart,
Like the music of that long decade

When some rush the stage to be nearer,
And some hold our breaths laughing.
Like the memory of that long decade
Speech trails out in hissing microphones.

And some hold our breaths laughing:
Ten minutes solemn as a power shortage.
Speech trails out in hissing microphones.
It is the time between off and on.

Ten minutes solemn as a power shortage,
Ten minutes of silence for John Lennon.
It is the time between off and on:
Death by signature, by the hand of love.

PAUL CELAN

"I hear that the axe has flowered,"
you said. It must have been
a furious bloom, for the chips that flew
to heal you, and then lie
soft and harmless on your collar.

It must have been a flowering
when the train rolled
from its tunnel, led by a shaft
of the purest light, as if
goodness could roll from the grave.

Your parents, riding that train,
could not have foreseen
an axe gone crazy, glinting
black, an axe that would salt
and eat its own handle.

Was it impossible for you
in Paris, lecturing
to children of the dead?
Did I hear you sift down
like chalk dusting a classroom?

Under a desktop in the last row
your initials deepen.
But I will have to stop saying
"Imagine Celan, who killed himself."
Everyone kills himself.

A LOT OF BOYS BAR

A lot of good boys got bad luck —
a jukebox parable you sing off the beat.
You forget that in your glistening eye
beer bottles stand as in a class photo,
the door to the ladies room opens wide,
and absolutely no one comes out smiling.

I'll buy you a drink despite your glare.
I am miserable too, and also mean.
A lot of poor boys turn mean —
bad family, bad cards, faces lumpy as wallets.
I'll tell you the story of my car wreck,
and then you tell me about yours.

I'm not lonely so much as bored into kindness.
You sat far from the TV end of the bar,
far from the looping pinball beat. I like that.
A lot of fine boys can't help themselves —
so dull they nose out sullen friends,
sit at dark tables, sneak looks at the waitress.

I'll tell you, today I stood on a sidewalk
at the battered pay phone reeking of small change,
and I heard brakes squeal uncontrollably.
For a minute I thought I was crashing again,
and couldn't stop laughing. A lot of good boys
like to ride on past their own braveries.

THE BAD CHILDHOOD OF CLAY

Mom hides sugar daddies.
Clay won't dare swipe one:
knowing a secret is worse than stealing.
She says, "Sweet tooth,"

hugs him tight like a wrapper
hidden in the wrong cupboard.
When he's older, he thinks,
his room will lock, and Dad

won't climb the stairs toward him.
Clay punches a sofa cushion
into a face with one eye.
These are secrets because he is bad,

won't sing Silent Night for the tape,
chucks a cat off the barn roof.
Clay thinks: the bad child
dreams because he is bad,

not because the house mumbles
and the furnace suddenly kicks on.
He thinks he'll soon be purely bad,
which will be no secret:

he'll dig the garden, tearing roots
with the blade of Dad's shovel.
They'll bleed like the arm of Clay
pushed through the back door screen.

CLAY'S GUN

Clay puts out the floodlit barn with a .22 —
raises dust on a hide
stretched to dry against the wall.
He can go off suddenly,
flare like a match head in a loft.

A deer shakes his tree-shaped head
against the leaves, runs from the light
Clay casts into the ditch.
Headlights of a junked car
shine in his flashlight beam.

He sees the city set on a hill,
sees it from his whole length
stretched in the front seat
waving his shadow hand
through moth clouds and junebugs.

In the city they will say
ride herd on your children,
but Clay has a gun and an eye
for targets, likes to kick up dust
in the road behind cars.

And at night he roams farm to farm
up the slopes toward town,
spooking dogs and cattle,
skipping chips of slate across fire ponds
to shatter the bedded moon.

At dawn he will run across mowed lawns,
curbs and gutters of the city,
and like a streetlamp he will stand
obvious on corners. Or
he may slip through the hedges —

in the city set on a hill, Clay
won't age like the moss-cracked sidewalks,
tar bubbling on a roof,
trophy head at a restaurant
whose nose is rubbed smooth by children.

CLAY'S HISTORY OF LOVE

Like someone who's never hungry
when observed, Clay roots
in a hedge of wild twigs,
crushed cones, and the rain
of yesterday's thunder.

There are lies he'd only tell
to himself, of home being dug
summerlong, how he'd play
in the mud, cross planks,
throw stones in pooled water

so that the unrisen house
would shimmer into view.
And a lie cements this day
to the next, makes it shudder
like a house when a tree falls,

knocking a gutter in the lawn
still visible by moonlight.
Clay thinks his girlfriend
must be blind, when she says yes
and meets his turned eyes.

They climb into the great hedge
and he shows her the sweet leaves
he has brought for them to lie on.
What if Clay cannot
tell the lies apart? —

ones he has heard, ones he's told,
ones he has mixed so well
with the truth. Clay thinks,
as she lifts her shirt tails free,
the whole farm must go blind.

CLAY'S ODD HOUSE

Many years beyond any reunion
Clay remembers the odd house he visited,
chips of glass, softening floors, speckled paint.
A graveyard grew among wild appletrees.

Where are the stupid pheasants on his way,
30-30 on his shoulder, wet mornings
all the way into October? Where
on the abandoned farmroad is the peace of Clay?

A fondness for secrets made Clay a boy
beyond boyhood: the tumbledown house
barely commanded a clearing
when Clay came hunting his past lives.

No one else came, but it wasn't
because the place was unknown.
Even Clay had to be led there at first,
some deerhunt with father and uncles.

Unlike them he kept the secrets
meant to be passed on, trivial
as this old house where two trails fork
at the secret center of Clay's forest.

III. Testament of Arnaud du Tilh

TESTAMENT OF ARNAUD DU TILH

*(Executed in 1560 in Gascony, France, for
impersonating Martin Guerre, who had
deserted his home and family a decade before)*

Still: call me Martin Guerre, this man
I became by fiat, by luck,
by the gift of my vast memory.
Wasn't that foolish, to believe
a wife wouldn't recall the least
motion of his hands, the way he

cast his eye about a new place?
The foolish frequently happens.
Whether I clear my throat or sigh
deeply, that other Martin dogs
me. I can never be alone.
Let the village squabble over

shoes, scars, broken teeth, and stories
of the Devil in sheep's clothing —
Martin Guerre, first born son of a
first born son, will inherit all.
In the marriage bed our laughter
was not forced, though my wife Bertrande

found me changed: more gracious, gentle,
talkative than I was. Two Me's
collide each day in a marriage:
do you think that's unusual?
Clever, I argued evidence
all day. But does the sky admit

evidence? Will the rich earth be
convinced? Can the pot of water
dispute the senseless touch of flames?
This day I, Arnaud du Tilh, known
as "Pansette," having persuaded
Martin Guerre's wife and kin to

accept me as her true husband,
having accepted myself the tasks
and joys of this life equally,
and having entered the thirty-third
and final year of my earthly
life, set down here the truth of truths.

True: I was a rogue on a rogue's
mission, arriving in these fields
with pockets empty and lungs full
of lies. True: I would have been gone
in a week, a little richer
with any luck, but for Bertrande,

who loved me at once for what I
therefore became. Also true: that
rogue, Martin, was not coming back.
If good springs from evil, honey
from the angry hive, must it be
condemned utterly? I was good

to her, and she loved me without
stint. I would not call her foolish,
for my lies were well told and most
needed. My well-performed deceit
became my earnest life. And didn't I
work? Didn't the wheat fields prosper?

Didn't I give another son
to keep the land *he* abandoned,
that father betraying his own?
How may I think of my mistake
but as kindness: to be myself,
fond husband remembering all?

Though it's right to forget some things
shouldn't a husband know which?
Let this then be my testament
to faithful and faithless alike
on whom my death may lay some claim,
for as I was wicked I was

the firm custodian of that
wickedness we call The World, which
I did not steal, though I held it.
To my false sisters that I love
better than my own, I bequeath
hope of good husbands arriving

down the rutted path that begins
at the farthest edge of their faith.
To my sons both natural and true
I leave the dust in my pockets
and whatever warmth they may find
in telling my tale to their sons.

As for my accusers, all but
Bertrande — let the wolves discover
their bones before they are quite cold,
and let them each be delivered
into such mercy as they showed
me, for I am a just liar.

Let honesty tempered with love
be a text they now remember.
And to the fields themselves, I leave
the muscles I bruised working them,
the grain that will flow from my hair,
and small stones of my blasphemies

for boys to toss at each other
whenever grownups aren't looking.
To my double, this grim Martin
Guerre, who hobbles now in judgment,
who has deserted wife, son, hearth,
family, and land of his birth,

who claims all now, with my own neck
for interest — I leave this name,
if he wants it back. Let him be
Martin Guerre again, the coward,
once I am smoke and ash that the
priest inscribes on sinful foreheads.

Let him seize this war name again:
we'll meet in flames in a simpler world.
We'll see which Martin Satan claims.
At last, Bertrande, the wife I call
mine even unto this sentence
of flame, whose misguided lover

I was and am, whose forgiveness
I do not demand — let her have
pardon though she is in no need.
I pardon her for not pardoning
me. I leave her good memories,
I trust, as she labors beneath

the weight of the husband she loved
more in duty than otherwise.
I bequeath her anything but
the sight of me swinging from the
gibbet, the fire crackling below.
I leave her my truest history.

For I will alter now, fable
among fables, according to
the teller. Hear me one last time:
Arnaud du Tilh hereby pleads guilty
to sacrilege, deception, and
love. If Heaven cannot abide

two men with one name, nor a wife's
will to choose, and choose again, then
let Heaven revise this story.
For myself, let hellfire be my
honeymoon. I almost welcome
the end of lies. The fields will be

lustrous this year, for there is peace
in the unwavering sun, strength
in wind and rain, righteousness in
obeying the seasonal law.
Whoever I will be, whether
Martin or Arnaud, I ask peace.

IV. The Library of Home

AMERICAN GOTHIC

I was christened from a telephone directory,
because my parents wanted a name no one had,
at least in this family. My first word was "bug."
Left in my playpen to drool and chatter
I posed stuffed animals for imaginary photos.
Soon I was singing songs invented
according to traffic signs. I loved
"yield," "go stop slow," and "squeeze left,"
all of which were possible in the back seat.
Down by the railroad tracks I churned hot gravel
fist to fist, awaiting the five-car freight.
In stores downtown I said "Charge it"
and my father's name. My school grades
were printed in the daily newspaper.

Mom kept her old address book a secret,
hidden under her voluminous underwear
in a dark oak dresser. Of course I peeked,
I was meant to, but I do not think
I was supposed to fall in love
with the brown-gray photos of that college girl,
strange as late night movies. I was young
but her truth was younger. And Dad
kept his secrets some place I never found,
though it's possible I didn't look hard,
as I turned away my eyes each time
he rose dripping from the bathtub.

And if I memorized sex manuals,
and if I caressed pillows and
practiced kissing mirrors, I can't remember.
What I remember are the dogs,
Eager, Loyal, and Foolish — teaching them
to worship the hoops they leaped through.

THE LIBRARY OF HOME

Refreshing to hear a familiar name
has gone under in the old home town,
or perhaps a bar where I once drank beer
and argued a position I hated.
My savings bank gives me the time of day,
Too Late, and the temperature, Very Low.
I remember what I love and no more:
I love a small town just after midnight,
when all the stoplights begin blinking "go,"
and the lit and empty telephone booths
begin their secret ringing in the fog.
A man wants his boyhood to be simpler:
even the headline's lie of omission
should comfort: honor roll, marriage, and death.
A never finished highway occupies
dotted lines on the map, like the unlived life
of the prodigal son, who would not fulfill
the provincial brag. The evening paper
headlines instead, "Man Gets What He Deserves,"
topic of every graduation speech.
A house I once lived in, altered and wrong,
succumbs to this bodiless longing, these
swirls of an unrecorded fingerprint.
Any snapshots curl their wings like dead moths
and turn slowly to dust in these attics,
a strangely ominous fidelity.
Any brain is folded upon itself
many times, like the chalkiest roadmap
still refusing to go the wrong way.
For here is a town whose mayor is part-time,
whose children orbit with glad gravity,
whose downtown will never move to the malls.
And at the library it is business
as usual, Andrew Carnegie's strange gift
to the heartland. Though on the street out front

the rubber skid-patches are permanent,
as is the dusting of shattered bottles
over the sidewalk, and though the aisles
are crowded with cookbooks and mysteries,
everyone knows there is a private shelf
in the librarian's office. And there
are the books of which I have always heard,
books of travel, lust, and complication.

EXITS ON THE DRIVE HOME

Sleet ahead freshens
the trees — hitchhikers
on the shoulder expect no rides,
but lean in the wash of wind

from my car. They are
the air from the vent
I hear hissing along my arm.
A bloodhound calls

from her chickenwire cage
beneath the apple tree.
I think of a house
whose son won't sleep

till he finds the hemlock
where he was conceived.
Here is a town of closed stores
and green lights turning greener.

I feel the gooseflesh
of cemetery lawns,
sons enrolled in brass
on the common,

bulls in paddocks,
moody in their sleep,
in that one town ahead
where no one has given up.

WIDOW'S QUILT

1

Jeep tracks die in the trees.
This road leads only home.
At last the woods give way
to rows of broad-lawned houses.

Once a pack of wild dogs came from the woods
and killed foals, tore the legs
of a horsebreeder waving his pitchfork.
If you do a thing like that you'd better mean it.

New here, I'd better learn
why the lone white church is empty,
learn not to pay any mind
to the cracked-up farmer standing in weeds,

flycasting high into his driveway.
This town is a widow's quilt,
forest shrinking, patches of corn and hay,
raccoon eyes vanishing in the pines.

2

Chuck holes, bent rake tine, sun high:
nothing was right in the garden that day.
Spotted adder slept in poison ivy,
by the soft place on the road shoulder

that claimed wheels to the hub. A quick sting:
wasp venom puffed my hand,
my spade clacked to the ground.
Grandfather came to press comfrey

to the sting. His breath smelled
of black birch, and he told me
how he once hooked an ear flyfishing,
never felt a thing with comfrey.

3

At the wreck, towtruck men gather,
dab a word or two in warm oil
across a caved-in door. A sweater
lies curled on the back seat.

A glance into some cars is like looking
in a bedroom where sheets rise.
The metal whines, straightening.
Moon hardens the outline

of the tomato stakes. On our road
a brown cloth fills with air
from the wind of a passing car,
rises toward anyone like a blindfold.

COW COUNTRY

The escaped cow wallows in a ditch near the wire-break,
stunned by traffic, by the circling dogs and family.
For acres, boulders asleep in pastures are cattle,
and pickups spin chaff into oncoming windshields.

She bellows worse than at a weaning.
Boys, up to their knees in muck, poke her with sapling poles.
During these storms they dream of bullheads
caught squirming in the elms around their cornfields,
and lakeweed everywhere on the shed roofs.

But on the road now the mud washes down,
hoofmarks vanish across gully and river bank —
a slope nearly too steep to drive any cow back up,
with water rising now to the guardrails.

So forget this farm, this long curve on Route Four,
this silo near full and brewing its own poison.
Forget all this as you drive
and you forget the first splutter of rain on your windshield,
the day the bridge collapsed beneath a log truck,
you forget the foaming collie shot once over a dead calf.

You forget almost nothing of this long afternoon
of sky darkening, of no cow missing, or ever missing,
by the time river hits the road.

THE OUTSKIRTS OF EVERYTHING

Sunday, every church is its own one-way street,
as every teacher alone in a classroom
draws furiously on the board with red chalk.
If there is anything noble in this town
it is the courthouse flag run to half mast
because we lost a couple dozen voters
between this census and the last, both rigged.
Let us come to such an altar to misbehave,
a town with torn sweatshirts waving from the stands,
a town ungovernable for its leashed and penned dogs.
Yet there is nothing especially settled here
despite the streets named after presidents
and extinct trees, despite the new reservoir
defeated by an immovable graveyard,
despite the library with its constant warp
in the fiction rack. Such friendship as will take
happens early and with the gravity of chance.
I should give my car keys to the nearest boy
who seems dazzled enough by the movie marquee.
I should wipe the smudges from the windows
of the police station, and stand revealed.
But behind the old-style grille at the bank
a teller wearing one of her mother's sweaters
begins to see in me my mother's myopic smile,
begins to call my bluff in simple questions
and careful, measured friendliness.
I know the spider in the vault is busy
among the stacks of long-cancelled checks
and think of him spinning with composure.

THE CLAY CALLED ENDURANCE
— for Lee

News from the storm, the power cutting storm —
Disneyland has been evacuated,
so much does fantasy depend upon
proper switchings of electricity.

And all across the country, from Portland
to Portland, the blank gray of traffic signals
makes no suggestions to us at all.
Here, it's earthworm weather, gray and sodden,

from here to the limit of our voices.
Isn't the genetic squirm appalling?
We say, *I haven't the foggiest notion,*
meaning that we do. These gray curls of life,

these worms appearing out of dismal mist,
do no harm but clutter our easy speech
with treacherous syllables. We dodge them
despite ourselves, till we are earthly too.

So breathe in this new fog, breathe out the old.
Then inside, we know the rain of events
must include us regardless, like the scrap
of news the paper imprints on a hand.

It's Easter. For drunken drivers, for crowds
awaiting the Pope, for the cross-eyed boy
balancing an egg on his outstretched spoon —
it's Easter all over the front page.

Various fires burn their way past the rain,
into the inner pages, where actors frown
in court, earthquake survivors turn the dirt,
and funeral homes praise resurrection.

Crash kills ten, rebels clash, and rescuer
feels cheated of just reward. We're cheated
by numbers, by the bleed-through of each page
of ads headlining faith to the faithful.

But must long examples of luck be lucky?
Good health, marriage enduring, happiness
simple as clouds afloat upon nothing
but themselves? Yesterday, walking Clay Street,

we spoke of any debris we came to.
A half crushed plastic bottle in the ditch
was rich with life that sour water allows.
I kicked it to see what violence does

in a small way. We had no camera
to record our interest. Two turkeys
at roost in a maple bobbed their red necks
to see us less. A collapsing gray shed

we've heard kids call haunted held on to the light
as I held you. The first colors of spring
were at the fringes of things, a few weeds
we failed to identify by the fence.

Imagine the clay called endurance,
I didn't say then. We passed a puddle
that rain or not seems deep and black. At night
I'm sure it swirls with mirrored galaxies.

Tonight, rain merciless and renewing,
as I let the newspaper hit the floor.
Sleep well, I think, not in preparation
or flight, but steadily as the rainfall.

Call it luck — even that may be endured.

ELEGY AT SEA

Cousin, you lie well cradled in the boat
you built yourself. The offcourse winds urged you
here to an island so remote that sand
is not so much white as difficult
to imagine. I think weed-wrapped turtles climb
from the waves near your hull. I think they drop
their rubbery eggs, bury them to bake
in the sand. The sky above your island
is the blue I remember tugging a kite
against my well-strung finger, stopping blood.

And that was cold but not so cold as dust
that lies at the heart of every raindrop.
Sun shower, smiled my father one day when
he taught me sand will bite when wind rouses,
surf spray eat the very roof off a car,
and in green waves floating jelly kills.
All this comes from the sky, as I understood
by the upturned face of my father, eyes
dipping and rising with the kite. Heart stopped,
cousin, you are bleachwood on a shore,
your mast pointing still as the wind allows.

When you fell to that deck you made a thump
I must be listening for. You would think
the sea would wash a last word free, a cry
riding waves as they lap the shoreline smooth.
It bothers me to know you as duty,
mere nod of the head at this service.
But it is your moorings that shift at night,
not mine, and you could never be sure what word
goes taut in the rigging. I am certain
only to cast this hurricane eye
against the horizon, dance in white sand,
and declare how the moon will die in surf.

LETTER TO KATHLEEN IN THE GREENHOUSE

The world of muteness: imagining this
is a pure terror, for a tongue is all
I have against the heart's cruel weathers,
or so I say, rehearsing misfortune
like a boy practicing fright in the mirror.
Kathleen, your tongue stilled by doctor's order
and surgical shock, I imagine you
sad, angry, gripping a severed phone cord.
No doubt I imagine wrongly. Silence
has its comforts, its vegetable strength.
The toad in the garden wears a jewel,
doesn't he? Isn't adversity sweet?
No, sweet are its *uses*, if you elect them,
as I would hope that you do, as I fear
I would not. Here the toad in my garden
is a clod of poisonous earth, making
dogs foam and children examine their skin
for warts, while the clouds of one storm disperse
and re-form, just as I had feared they would.
In your greenhouse the protected flowers
of far lands bloom with artificial rain —
you sketch them, rapt as a flower yourself,
listening as only the silent can.
In that humid warehouse of unwildlife,
that museum of tropic profusion,
you sit with head bent like a lady's slipper
capturing leaf, stem, sepal, and petal,
capturing your own focused attention
to the spendthrift creation of this world.
Are there any toads in that glassed garden?
I'd wish you the changeless weather of faith,
its well assorted, labelled specimens,
except that there are storms in a glass house,
there are blights and mishaps, even if fewer
than under the bare sky.
                              I simply trust

you will choose silence as it chooses you,
transparent eyes behind transparent walls.
The silent are not the meek, and may not
inherit anything, but they may thrive,
for they will know more of the names of things.
From my window I see milkweed, crown vetch,
redtop in waves down to a slope of oaks —
I send them to you now, name and body,
though if forced to choose I would give the names,
adding others I like: poverty grass,
timothy, wintergreen, skunk cabbage, rue.
And for you I would pick forget-me-not,
Kathleen's lost voice, and sweet everlasting.

FATHER MOVIES

In the movie the Angus cows
shuffle and shake off flies;
geese swim the pond,
half silted in now
and floating a rug of scum.
Pigs face a water hose
in the brown sun
drinking and grinning
while seven kids dance
dressed in mud near the father.

My father owned their farm,
but who could own a burning house,
a spume of ice
where hosewater hit the stones and froze?
They wrapped themselves in blankets,
that other family,
squinted in the snow
at blinking firetrucks.
Then they were gone
further into the white valley.

But those charred timbers,
bulldozed into the cellar,
rise again,
with their rolling floors,
while the mother
steers a tractor through the field
so that her husband,
home from a night job,
can sleep.

And my father
owned this palomino
taking the weathered fence
in slow motion,

these spaniels nipping
sled-runners on blue ice.
He owned our afternoons
stretching wire pole to pole
in knee-deep yellow grass,
or loafing in the loft
shooting the gray shadows
of pigeon and mouse.

Where is their beagle
tied to the porch,
or their lone Holstein, Snowball,
snuffing bare bellies
for another taste of salt?
Where is the overdue rent
passing hands,
or the rotted silo
on its way down,
or the whole brown field lit
and moving toward the pond?

My father shot everything
he wanted, and left out nothing
of the wind bending alfalfa
into green breakers,
or the willow that leans over water.
In the distance a car, old even then,
glints beneath a rearing horse.

THE MOVIE OF FUGITIVE LIFE

— after "The Third Man"

Imagine a city beneath
this city, a network of streets
upon which our own streets must thrive.
Imagine a sewer system
vast and complicated as life.
You would look in confusion there
from one passageway to the next,
voices and echoes everywhere,
just as in your uppermost life.
And the smell, of course, would be bad
as imagination required.
And if it were an old city
above your sewer, these tunnels
would be opulent, backlit with
wide walkways, and wrought iron rails
along the spiral staircases.

You could almost think a father
strolled these glistening cobblestones,
clacking his cane with father-pride,
or that a mother bathed her child
in one of these unquiet pools.
The household sounds of this chase scene
soon terrify the fugitive,
as anger is always the worst
when the upraised hand is your kin.
If you were to fire a gun here
the echoes would soon redouble
so that the source of violence
would be everywhere. It would be
complicated but familiar
to be fugitive here. A sound
in your ears fevering, viral.

And what is that dripping, dripping?
Is it the blood of homecoming
or of disaster? One sewer
divides and redivides, like time
itself, so there is no return
and you are being chased for good.
Don't think of the dark shops above,
the placid bakeries, fruit stands,
and newspaper racks. Here the news
is itself your sole nourishment,
and the news is that these tunnels
seem to have no end, but they do,
of course they do. An iron grate,
a glimpse of light from streets above.
Imagine this fugitive life
if you can think of no other.

WORCESTER, NEXT NINE EXITS

My waitress wipes her hands
and grows older.
As I leave, I overhear
the musical kitchen,

where my food returns
to be consumed.
Out back, crates give off
several childhood odors.

There's a place off the exit loop
where kids collect like rain
in a rock hollow that was
blasted by mistake.

They know the different makes
of truck, they predict
which cars hit the guardrails
ten miles on.

Turnpike ahead shimmers with glass.
Intelligent people have collided
with stupid ones. Where I'm going
caved roofs still hold back the rain,

flattened cans ascend to be filled,
a cat who has been given away
just makes it across the road
to the old neighborhood.

MAGIC SHOWS

1. *Legends of Jim*

For each new course Jim pulled the same coin
from a new ear. The chimp at the dinnertable
ate peas from a knife, ignoring manners
taught strictly by the maids. A black bear
lounged on his chain in the backyard,
dog-killer, soon to be given sadly to the zoo.
A boa curled in the cool tin bucket
around still-warm mouse and rabbit.
Perhaps a lone canary cage stood empty
for Lent — this man denied himself little,
denied his family less.

              Let's pretend
I remember, the life-size stuffed gorilla
he bought me at the carnival, where we gawked
at the freaks he loved. I sat in the lap of a man
fatter than Jim, who slipped a finger ring
over my whole hand. Then guessed my weight —
"puny," howling as Jim yanked me off
to feed the elephants despite four signs
wired to the bars. Will this freakshow
ever shrink to a book full of photos,
single page in the center with its three-legged calf?

Better to revisit his lakeside house
opened each summer, the kitchen aired,
and in the beds chestnuts we found
laid between mattress and coverlet.
Wild snakes sunning on the flagstone porch
could always slip into crumbling mortar.
Easy to imagine how inside becomes outside,
so that our headlights picked out eyes of raccoon
wide in the kitchen windows, and we found
all the hourglasses just turned.

At home, a trunkful of Jim's props
waited me out in our own attic —
rabbit-filled tophats, creaky boxes
that filled suddenly with rubber fruit.
I waved his threadbare silks for the dead mirror,
shuffled decks of fifty-two six-of-hearts.

Can I forgive his card sleights and coins
vanishing above my crib? He was Diamond Jim
in every album, grinning on the dais
handing a check to orphans, or for Halloween
dressed as the pirate with nothing left to steal.
Grandmother solved the problem of how to fill
his shoes — she let them loom in a closet
with a painting that had frightened him
so much he had to buy it.

But every trick in the book had his X
slashed in the margin. To a secretary
he scribbled "Get." I read the carbons
he kept in a vault like cufflinks,
clumsy and misspelled, as if to prove
his saying — nobody misreads a blank check.

Amateur, magician, big-tipper, he sailed
through the Depression in a three piece suit,
lord of the many course meal
and the bulging humidor, angry only
when the gardener forgot and called him Mister.
He never trusted the brakes of a car
he wasn't driving. Did he practice
in front of this mirror? Let's pretend
I remember his twisted knuckles, age-spotted skin
he never earned pulling eggs from a sleeve,
let's pretend this fat man loves me
peering from grandmother's nightstand with my wand.

2. *Home Movies, Circa 1935*

Twenty years after his death, I watch Jim
rise unsteadily, twenty years before that.
What I forgot, what I never saw —
it's all in movies my uncle made, flickering illusions
of the uncritical eye which is love.
Here is Jim's easy, tip-of-the-hat smile
to his daughter, my dead aunt Mary Lib,
as she helps him heave himself out of a car.
Fragment and accident live: Jim's face
briefly at a window, nervous fatherly smile,
my teenage mother on a go-cart, waving.
And that legendary menagerie is here,
we watch it enlarging from reel to reel —
alligators smaller than Jim's shoes, snapping toes,
and two or three chimps, no one can agree,
just as no one agrees on the names
of that pair of spaniels in the snowy street,
who lope uncurious past the camera.
And here is Jim tossing a baby chimp in the air
as I imagine he lobbed his newborn son.
He's rewarded now by a playful nip,
and unholy screeching fills the family room.

3. *My Magical Career*

Dazzled like any boy by the tasteless,
I took to his corny props with a devotion
that made grandmother smile wearily.
I sleighted long afternoons for any mirror,
dreaming myself in command of a narrow spot.
Though I'd been too young to see Jim perform
his hand lay unseen in all I did,
poring over yellowed instruction sheets,
learning moves more baffling than marriage manuals.
For the first time I made sense of my thumbs,
tutored each fold of skin for a miracle,
so that in time I might read coins by feel.

Jim's wallet also supported me, invisible
and prodigious as language. Grandmother bought me
flowing silks to replace his tattered ones.
If to this day illusion comforts more than irks me
I think it's not an insider's smirk
but a child's thirst for recurrence: peekaboo, Jim,
it amazes me still, how the nothing
from which a chosen card leaps to light
is always your same patch of worn velvet
that just grows more perfect by spotlight.

Chipped glossy paint, browning glue, Jim left
the doomed possessions of any householder,
though I cherished the hat that couldn't be worn,
matches that lit themselves and then vanished,
like Jim, leaving just their flames.

I wound up finding my own fraternity,
performing in lodge halls, church basements, schools,
testing Jim's books, chapters on Black Art and Misdirection.
The talk was called patter, though, and was my own,
for Jim's attic-born box of tricks was his tomb.

4. *Jim's Soldier Today*

This too-small man who stands among us,
whose head's too large and who's always staring,
is all foolishness, jug-eared and granite skulled,
clutching that stone gun to his rocky chest,
and smiling an idiot pre-war grin.
I think the ground he stands on must be firm,
isn't it? The riffling leaves of August
don't disturb his well-photographed composure —
for as long as I have known he's been here,
planted by the roadside with his rifle,
a grandfatherly whimsy, isn't he,
with his stone cap, marbled eyes and moustache?
Vandals tipped him over once, I recall —

that's how he got those chips in his trousers.
Riding down the hill toward him in the dark
I'd flinch every time as headlights swept him,
and his shadow leaped back into the woods
like a deer — anyone would have been scared
into malice by that. But as a boy
I saw soldiering without an army,
and vigilance so far from any front
it spooked grandmother, too, like a token
of her widowhood. Where this man came from
was as mysterious to me as where
my grandfather had gone. Now I wonder more
why he wanted this gray, clumsy relic
to guard his driveway, and why, ever since,
we have honored his wishes. Posing here
by this ever-posing figure, I'm glad
he stands among us, though what he stands for
is nothing more than family, nothing
but that allegiance anyone will claim.

5. *The Living Yoke*

That's him — forthright in snapshot frame,
genial eyes shaded with a boy's gloom,
a Thirties dandy in double-breasted coat,
complete with a twelve-foot constrictor
slung over his shoulders, a living yoke.

Jim squints a little — that's it, the light
too harsh for honesty here. A vine-clad
tile wall places him — no safari
but a zoo. No costume but pleasure.

Hard not to think of snake oil, the crisp barker
selling nothing but himself. Jim not a man
to refuse me, even after his death —
the house still rich with his leathery,
cigarsmoke breath, his vaporized cologne.

I loved the attic for its alien comfort,
a many-point buck staring down linen chests,
whose mothballs could not erase that gamy tang,
and the rolltop desk, with its crumbled receipts,
and the army dress sword, engraved
on each side with the same surrender.

Hard not to think his frantic collection
hid something, as Jim in albums was always
on vacation, always on stage, often
as not wearing someone else's hat.

Jim stood for whatever crept, swam, slithered
or flew, loving all with his baggy warmth
and pocketful of uncrinkled cash.
Still, with silk tie and archaic smile,
he bears these coiled scales. A snake can bite,
can curl to crush, but the venom
Jim should fear is this crooked devotion
of a grandson.

        Someone's hand steadies
the snake's wedged head, someone out of this picture —
and vanishes the more I stare at Jim
shouldering the weight, including his own.

ACQ2503

2/9/99
gg

PS
3557
R193
M3
1986